7 Rules That Can Save Your Life

Common Sense Self-Defense

David Garcia

Stewart Smith

Photography by

Peter Field Peck

10X 2/05 √9/05

HATHERLEIGH PRESS • New York • A GetFitNow.com Book

Printed in Canada
Designed by Rachel Reiss
Cover design Dawn Velez-LeBron

Published by Hatherleigh Press
An affiliate of W.W. Norton & Company, Inc.
5-22 46th Avenue, Suite 200
Long Island City, NY 11101

Library of Congress Cataloging-in-Publication Data
Garcia, David, 1959-
Common sense self-defense : 7 techniques that can save your life /
David Garcia, Stewart Smith ; photography by Peter Field Peck
p. cm.
"A GetFitNow.com book."
ISBN 1-57826-090-6 (paper : alk. paper)
1. Self-defense—Handbooks, manuals, etc. I. Stewart Smith, 1969- II. Title
GV1111 .G29 2002
796.81—dc21
2002068690

10 9 8 7 6 5 4 3 2 1

Common Sense
Self-Defense

Warning!

The contents of this book are not a substitute for proper training in self-defense and the martial arts. The material presented in this book is for information and entertainment only; by reading further you accept any and all responsibility for any damage and risk, psychologically and/or physically, to you and/or to someone else, that may result from the use or application of any information assimilated from this book. In consideration of reading this book and using its information, you waive all rights of damages against Stew Smith, Dave Garcia, Getfitnow.com, and Hatherleigh Press, and the officers, employees, associates, sub-contractors, and contractors of the above stated. It is recommended that you receive written permission from your doctor before commencing or increasing the intensity of any physical fitness program.

Dedication

To the men and women of the United States of America.
May they lead their lives in comfort and security.

Acknowledgements

The authors would like to express their thanks to Joseph LaFrance, who generously shared his expertise with us; Anne Stewart, who graciously gave up her time to pose for us; and Jim Thomas, who had the unfortunate task of playing the "villain" for the photos in this book. Special thanks also to Kevin Richard Reppenhagen and John Dove.

Contents

Preface

Date rape. Purse snatching. Carjacking. Mugging. Terrorism. This world can be a dangerous place. Now there is something you can do to protect yourself and your loved ones.

In your hands is an effective personal protection manual written by two of the top self-defense instructors in the world. It presents an intelligent approach to self-defense that anyone can use in times of trouble—spouse, daughter, mother, brother, sister.

Common Sense Self-Defense is the brainchild of former Navy SEAL Stewart Smith and former RECON Marine David Garcia. Dave Garcia is police detective and SWAT Team member and certified self-defense instructor for the police force. Stew Smith is fitness author and former self-defense instructor at the United States Naval Academy.

Common Sense Self-Defense is a basic program that takes only minutes a week to practice—as opposed to a Martial Arts program that takes several hours a day to master. It offers options, techniques, and a way of analyzing situations. This program will teach you seven effective physical techniques to help you survive almost any situation, and will also teach you ways to avoid potentially dangerous situations.

You will learn psychological awareness and non-verbal and verbal skills—giving you a greater sense of empowerment and self-assurance.

Common Sense Self-Defense will not only teach you how to effectively use your hands, elbows, knees, and feet as weapons, but also how to use your head—in more ways than one. Stew and Dave will walk you through training techniques, attacks and defense scenarios.

If you know very little about defending yourself, with this book you will learn the basics and enough to avoid or survive an attack.

Andrew Flach

Introduction

Common Sense Self-Defense, or CSSD, is an approach to personal protection for anyone who wants to learn basic self-defense, street-fighting techniques, and skills that may save his or her life. The CSSD program does not include any of the traditions common to martial arts. Nor does it require the enormous time commitment required becoming a martial arts master. Rather than creating complex choreographed fighting patterns, CSSD concentrates on full-contact hand-to-hand training as used by the military's SEAL teams and RECON Units.

We encourage anything that can help you survive, from knee and elbow strikes to head butting, biting, and eye gouging. When you are fighting for your life, you have one goal: **do whatever it takes to survive**.

You can very quickly achieve a high degree of proficiency because this program is founded on common principles and instinctive reactions that can be applied to multiple scenarios. All the techniques that are taught in this book are no-nonsense and reality-based; not techniques for sport competition. The only rule we follow is: THERE ARE NO RULES!

We are going to teach you to recognize the danger at the earliest possible stages. The techniques that we will show you can work from positions of disadvantage, stress, and surprise. They are easy to learn and easy to retain, and they can be performed from a passive state without hesitation.

Hostile situations are a fact of life. Our goal is to help prepare you mentally and physically to recognize and avoid a hostile situation by walking away or talking your way out of danger. However, if you are forced to fight, the combat tools in this book will help you to protect yourself from bodily harm.

Common Sense Self-Defense will instill confidence and teach you how to avoid becoming a victim. It uses the same techniques as the police force and the Special Forces of the United States Military. In police and military training, students do not have the time to become black belts, so the instructors teach the very best methods derived from the martial arts—a combination designed to overcome a wide variety of threats.

The basic techniques found in *Common Sense Self-Defense* do not require years of practice, but require only minutes of practice and review each week. You will learn first and foremost how to anticipate and avoid potentially dangerous, life threatening situations.

You will then learn how and what to strike. How to make a fist. Effective combinations of punches and kicks. Targets on your attacker's body that are especially vulnerable to defensive moves. If confrontation is unavoidable, **you will be able to react with confidence and force**.

Most importantly, you will learn to think defensively. More than anything else, your intellect will guide you safely through compromising situations. Whether it's staying out of risky environments, escaping before the encounter gets physically violent, or using your body as a weapon of self-protection as a last resource—your knowledge and training will determine the outcome.

Keep in mind that this book was not written for you to use to bully, cajole, threaten, or intimidate others. Nor is it the last word on self-defense. We recommend that you seek proper instruction with a knowledgeable CSSD instructor who can observe and coach you on proper hitting and blocking techniques.

David Garcia
Stew Smith

The Seven Rules of Self-Defense

Rule #1: Use Your Head

Rule #2: Avoid Danger

Rule #3: Know When to Use Force

Rule #4: Know How to Hit

Rule #5: Know What to Hit

Rule #6: Know How to Fight

Rule #7: Train for Self-Defense

Rule #1: Use Your Head

Rule #2: Avoid Danger

Rule #3: Know When to Use Force

Rule #4: Know How to Hit

Rule #5: Know What to Hit

Rule #6: Know How to Fight

Rule #7: Train for Self-Defense

Chance Favors Those Who Are Prepared

Every 60 seconds, someone is assaulted in the United States. The odds are high that you might be involved in a violent incident some time in your life. Crime knows no bounds—it crosses all social and ethnic lines. It is a fact that we can choose to ignore . . . or we can be ready for it.

Many Americans live in fear of crime. Behind closed doors they lock their lives. Perhaps they have been victims themselves, or know a friend or relative who was attacked, beaten, robbed, or worse. And so they go about their lives never knowing when they will be next.

Others take a proactive approach. They take a self-defense course at a local Y or community education center. They learn how to avoid dangerous people and places. They practice defensive maneuvers designed to disable an attacker. They know when to flee and when to fight. They take self-protection seriously and can approach life with confidence and courage. Not that they are fearless . . . no, just the opposite. They understand fear, know the risks, and have the courage to overcome their fear when their lives are threatened.

And so, the first rule of self-defense: use your head. Be proactive in your approach to personal protection and safety. Reading a book like this will give you valuable insights into how you can minimize your exposure to risky environments and increase your ability to survive a fight if that is what it takes.

Ignorance is no excuse. You must take responsibility for your own safety in this world. Sure, there are police officers and security guards that will help deter crime. But they can't be everywhere! You need to use your head to and learn about areas of your town or city that should be avoided. You need to avoid behavior that can put you at risk of being victimized. **You need to learn how to use verbal and non-verbal skills to ward off a potential attacker.**

And you must learn to fight for your life.

Think Positive

Your mind is your primary weapon, so stay low-key and don't look for trouble. Maintain a positive mental attitude. It is said your body is capable of ten times more than your mind believes it to be–so don't limit yourself by underestimating your capabilities. Keep an open mind. Ask questions and continue to learn. The key to survival is developing awareness, self-control, and a fighting spirit.

Fighting is ugly. Violent, angry people are unpredictable. Expect the worst—when threatened with violence, anticipate an immediate and overwhelming attack. Expect the unexpected—just because you don't see a weapon, don't assume that your attacker is unarmed. If he is alone, expect others to join him. Expect maximum resistance—don't underestimate your attacker.

Remember: a self-defense program is only as good as the person using it. You have to have an offensive mindset to survive and attack and then use only enough force to stop the immediate threat. In the streets there is no such thing as a fair fight, and there are no rules or timeouts. Use every means at your disposal to avoid getting injured.

Avoiding a conflict situation is your best bet. Always ask yourself, "Am I willing to get hurt for this?" or "Is this worth hurting somebody for?" Usually, you can answer these questions very logically.

The next time someone takes your parking spot or bumps into

you at a bar, think twice before starting a fight. People have been killed over less.

But if the moment comes when you have to engage an attacker, use your head to take command of the situation and use the skills you will discover in the pages ahead.

Avoidance: Your Best Defense

Situational Avoidance Strategies

The best way to defend against danger is to avoid danger in the first place. Whether in your car or on foot, at home or work, with friends at a bar or on a date, there are specific things you can do to reduce your exposure to attack.

Why increase your chances of being victimized when you can do something about it?

Keep in mind: this does not mean you are living in fear and having your life limited or otherwise controlled by the wanton acts of criminals. Rather you are choosing to stay out of harm's way. That is an intelligent, reasonable, and sensible choice. To go forewarned into trouble is a foolish choice.

The following pages present some common crimes and ways you can protect yourself from harm.

ATM Machines

Automated Teller Machines (ATM) have made access to our banking system convenient twenty-four hours a day. Whether for a withdrawal or deposit, transfer or balance review, ATMs have become a part of our daily lives. ATMs also happen to be a favorite target for muggers. They smell money. Most likely you will be alone and vulnerable, with your wallet or purse open and access to quick cash just a crime away. ATMs are a watering hole for lurking attackers. And you are fair game to them.

TIPS TO AVOID THIS ATTACK:

■ **Watch for suspicious persons**

Always check the area around an ATM for suspicious persons before and during ATM use. Even in broad daylight with plenty of people around, you can become a victim of robbery if you're not careful. If you see someone standing around or watching you intently, do not attempt to withdraw any money. Go to another ATM location. Always look around at your surroundings before, during, and after your visit to the ATM. Stay alert until you return to your vehicle.

■ **If you have a car**

Do not leave your vehicle engine running or doors unlocked while you use an ATM, when anyone could easily enter your vehicle and steal it. Park your vehicle at a reasonable distance from the ATM.

■ **Keep your ATM activity brief and secure**

Make certain to have your ATM card available before you approach the ATM. Memorize your PIN number (Do not write your PIN number on your ATM card). Get your ATM transaction done quickly. Don't stand around counting your money or balancing your checkbook at the ATM location. If you arrive at an ATM that appears to have been tampered with, don't use the machine. Leave the ATM area quickly and contact the police.

■ **Give charitably elsewhere**

There are many worthy charitable organizations where your money is needed and can do good works. Giving to a panhandler who is stationed near the ATM is not helping . . . in fact you could be inviting a crime. Rather, do not stop. Do not give panhandlers any money. Say no politely and continue on your way. If the panhandler is aggressive, move away from them quickly. Report his or her actions to the police as soon as possible.

Purse Snatch/Hold-up

Let's face it. Nothing in your purse or wallet is worth risking your life for. A set of keys? A hairbrush? A pack of gum? Your credit cards? Your dignity?

Bottom line: if it comes down to turning these items over to a criminal or facing uncertain harm, give them up. Property can be replaced; your life can't.

TIPS TO AVOID THIS ATTACK:

- **Take only what you need**

  Don't carry a purse when you don't need to. If possible, lock your purse in the trunk of a vehicle. Carry only the amount of money you need, or your credit card, and an identification card.

- **Travel smart, Travel safe**

  When carrying your purse, try to hold it in front of you, rather than out to the side where a person can attempt to grab the straps or the purse itself. When walking, try to walk with another person or a small group. Be aware of who's around you as you walk. Always keep your purse close to you; don't set it down in an open area. Don't open your purse and search through it as you are walking outside. Don't allow strangers to distract you or confuse you. Keep walking, but stay alert. Report any suspicious behavior to the police.

- **Keep your valuables in a safe place**

  Don't leave home with your worldly wealth in a handy "take out" package. Keep photocopies of your credit cards, social security card, health insurance cards, and driver's license at home in a safe place. In the event your purse or wallet is lost or stolen, you can quickly alert the proper authorities and avoid needless expense and inconvenience.

Sexual Assault

Rape and other forms of sexual assault are the most cowardly and vicious of crimes. Rape is usually perpetrated by a physically stronger individual against a physically weaker individual—whether a woman, a man, or a child. Women fear sexual assault more than any other crime because sexual assault can harm a woman physically, emotionally, and psychologically. That is why you must avoid any and all situations where a potential sexual assault is likely.

TIPS TO AVOID AN ASSAULT:

- **Protect yourself from strangers**
  A smiling face can hide a deceitful mind. Don't put yourself into compromising situations with strangers. Don't accept car rides from strangers. If a friend can't pick you up and you have no money for a taxicab, call the police. They will make sure you get home safely.

- **Exercise safely**
  Parks, though beautiful, can be dangerous places, especially at odd hours and in remote locations. If you like to run for exercise, choose not to jog in secluded areas or alone. Instead, join a runner's club and jog with others. Don't push your luck and run at early in the morning or late at night, when the park is deserted. Run when the trails are full, not empty. And keep your portable stereo at home. With music blasting in your ears, chances are you won't hear a rapist approaching. Nor a car for that matter.

- **Stay sober, stay alert**
  Don't abuse alcoholic beverages or take drugs that cause you to lose control of your actions—and allow others to take advantage of you. Date rapes usually involve drugs or alcohol. Keep your wits about you and use common sense.

Home Intrusion or Break-in

Home Intrusion or Break-in

Home intrusion or burglary is a very serious problem due to the drug problem in today's society. Nearly everyone arrested for burglary–both male and female–has an illegal drug habit. Most remaining burglaries are either domestic or by a known person.

Drug abusers will break into a home or business and steal property—money, jewelry, cell phones, cameras, and lap top computers—which can be traded or sold for illegal narcotics.

When confronted, drug abusers and other burglars can be very dangerous. So do what you can to deter them in the first place!

TIPS TO AVOID THIS ATTACK:

- **Protect your home**

  Keep your doors and windows locked at all times, even during the day—especially if no one is going to remain at home. Use curtains and shades so that no one can look inside. Use motion sensors on your outside lights, targeting the back yard, any secluded area, or any area that faces the woods. If you can afford it, get an alarm system or a dog.

- **Mind your keys**

  Don't leave spare keys under your door mat. Don't be forgetful and leave your house key inside your front door knob. Why make it easy for someone to walk right in?

- **Don't let strangers in your house**

  Keep all unknown people outside! If a person knocks on your door and asks to use your phone because his car broke down, don't let him inside. Instead, offer to call the police for him. Report to the police any suspicious people attempting to gain entry into your home.

- **Watch for unusual behavior**

  Pay attention to unusual people or activity your neighborhood. Organize a Crime Watch with your neighbors. If you hear unusual noises coming from your neighbor's home, alert the police. Your home could be next.

Carjacking

Carjacking is a robbery involving the theft of a vehicle, where force or the threat of force is used against the driver or occupants of the vehicle. Carjackers can be very dangerous and desperate criminals. And if you choose to drive a vehicle that is worth the price of a small house, you are asking for trouble. Don't let your conspicuous consumption become a lure for crime!

TIPS TO AVOID THIS ATTACK:

- **Keep your car secure**
  Keep your vehicle doors locked at all times, day or night, and even while you're driving. Don't leave your vehicle engine running or your vehicle unsecured inside as you run inside a store for a quick errand. Never leave children in an unattended car.

- **Minimize your exposure**
  Pay attention to what's going on around you. Don't pick up hitchhikers. Don't pick up strangers who claim that their vehicle has broken down; instead, call the police so they'll get help. If you see suspicious persons near your vehicle, do not approach it. Stay away and notify the police or security.

- **Keep a cell phone handy**
  Cell phones can be a valuable deterrent to carjackings. In the event of an accident on the road, no matter how minor, stay in your car and call the police immediately. Give them your location. Do not leave your car if the location is deserted or unsafe . . . unless your car is on fire or filled with smoke.

Bar Fight

People who frequent bars like to drink. And under alcohol's influence, bar patrons can lose control. They can become rude, threatening, and aggressive. They may be a friend or a stranger. They may be stressed or angry and when triggered, they may rage into an uncontrollable fury. While it may be best to stay away from bars and nightclubs, for most of us it is impractical as these places are common social environments. But there are things you can do to avoid being on the receiving end of a drunkard's attack.

TIPS TO AVOID THIS ATTACK:

■ **Watch the crowd**

In a bar or nightclub, stay away from people that you think may be trouble. If upon arrival you feel uncomfortable or threatened by the "look" of the crowd, walk out and find another destination. Don't give in to peer pressure to stay.

■ **Keep cool**

If you notice a person across the room looking at you, don't glare back. If someone stares at your date or spouse, don't get angry. If it gets too uncomfortable, alert the bartender or bouncer. And don't start trouble yourself by abusing alcohol to a point where you can't control your own actions.

■ **Set limits**

Physical touching is a serious matter. If you find yourself in a situation where a person is grabbing at you or your date, attempt to alert the bartender or bouncer. Let them handle the situation for you. Usually, if the staff has any difficulty, they will call the police.

Road Rage

Just because someone has a license to drive a car and has never been a criminal before doesn't mean they won't commit an act of violence commonly referred to as road rage. Road rage is a bizarre and dangerous by-product of our modern world. Endless traffic jams and the pressure of daily life creates a highly volatile, and sometimes lethal, cocktail of violence.

Triggered by a minor fender bender or a honking horn, the road rager can go berserk and attack without notice. Driving a vehicle on the roadway gives most people a false sense of security. The truth is you are very vulnerable to road rage.

TIPS TO AVOID THIS ATTACK:

- **Avoid aggressive drivers**

  Do not get involved with anyone that drives in an aggressive manner. Allow an aggressive driver to pass you. Don't play games with him or her; it's not worth it. Use your cell phone to report an aggressive driver to the police by giving the vehicle license plate number and a basic description of the driver.

- **If you are in an accident**

  Stay calm and get a good look at the other driver. Close your windows and lock your doors. Memorize or write down the other driver's vehicle license number in case he tries to leave, and don't make any statements or argue with him about who is at fault. Call the police; stay at the scene until they arrive. If the other driver starts to approach you with an angry, threatening look or a possible weapon, leave the scene immediately.

DOMESTIC VIOLENCE

If problems with domestic violence occur repeatedly, become more frequent, or get worse, you need to ask yourself: is it worth staying in this relationship? Sometimes, for the sake of your safety and sanity, you need to cut your losses and move on. You cannot force a person to change or to seek help if he doesn't want to. Most police departments no longer tolerate domestic violence and will help in any way they can. Usually, the offender will be placed under arrest.

The victims of domestic violence can include women, children, the elderly, and men. Perpetrators of domestic violence include husbands against wives, wives against husbands, parents against children, children against adults, nurses against patients. Surprised? Don't be. Domestic violence affects us all.

TIPS TO AVOID THIS ATTACK:

- **Keep a safe distance**

  Don't place yourself in a position where you can be physically assaulted. Always walk away from a heated argument. If your spouse is intoxicated and abusive, make arrangements for one of you to stay somewhere else until your spouse has sobered up and cooled off.

- **Use monitoring devices**

  If you suspect a family member is being battered in your absence, whether it be by another family member or a babysitter or nursing professional, do not hesitate to set up a remote video camera and review the tape. If it reveals abusive action, contact the police.

- **Get help**

     Don't hesitate to contact the police if you need help. Seek counseling or crisis support groups. Whatever you do, don't be silent about it. Don't be ashamed (or afraid) to seek help for you and your family.

Some General Verbal and Non-Verbal Avoidance Guidelines

Just as it is possible to avoid dangerous situations, it is also possible to diffuse potential threats by using verbal cues and body language to dissuade your would-be attacker. If you feel threatened, use the following tips to keep the situation from becoming physical.

- Use loud, confident words to startle your attacker: "stop!"

- Make eye contact. Maintain eye contact. Eye contact is a powerful statement of self-confidence.

- Agree with the aggressor; concede; converse for an understanding.

- Maintain control of yourself and the situation. Even if you are scared to death, don't show it. Do not lose your cool, argue or yell.

- Look confident, not scared. Body language goes a long way: stand tall, with your head up and your shoulders back. Don't look down, stare, or suddenly look away. This is the body language of someone intimidated and scared.

- Don't look back in a challenging manner. Be confident, but do not cross the line and appear challenging to an attacker. Do not challenge or threaten.

- Never talk back in a challenging or threatening manner. Be firm and assertive, but do not talk back in a manner that may give the aggressor an excuse to escalate the situation.

- Be assertive and quick. Say what you mean and mean what you say.

- Say "no" many times loudly. Be firm, talk loudly, and draw the attention of others to the situation.

- Maintain control of the conversation. Control the conversation; control the situation.

- Do not laugh or embarrass the aggressor.

- Maintain a safe distance at all times.

- Never give away personal information. Do not tell strangers your name, your destination, etc.

Again, however, it is best to avoid dangerous situations altogether than to find yourself arguing with a potential attacker.

Making the Decision

Assess the Situation

No matter how hard you try to avoid dangerous situations, there is always a chance that you will find yourself the target of a criminal attack. If that should happen, you might be confronted with a decision: should you use force to defend yourself?

THE LAWS OF SELF-DEFENSE

- Usually the law allows you to use deadly force (any force which could cause serious physical injury or death) to protect yourself and others when you reasonably believe you are threatened with immediate serious bodily harm or death.

- If you use force, use only the amount of force necessary to neutralize the attack. You will have to justify the level of force you used according to the level of threat that was present.

- If an aggressor gets too close or you feel your safety is threatened with immediate physical harm, try to run, leave, or get help—or, if you feel you have no other option and are sure that your attacker does not have a weapon, make the decision to fight.

The Element of Surprise

Usually, the decision to attack occurs within seconds, so if you are forced to fight you should immediately begin looking for available target striking points. Your goal is to strike first in an attempt to end the fight before it begins, so if you choose to strike, strike hard, furiously and effectively. This gives you the element of surprise and, believe it or not, it is considered self-defense.

If you feel threatened, you CAN strike first. Surprise the attacker by not taking a defensive stance—this will only alert your attacker that you may fight. Attack while your attacker still thinks he or she has the advantage.

Always try to end the fight as soon as possible to avoid any chance of serious injury or death. By taking the offensive in an attack, you gain the element of surprise, and hopefully control the situation. Whatever

Should I use force?

Answer "yes" to these questions first.
- Is there imminent danger?
- Does this person intend to harm me?
- Is the number of attackers small enough for me to handle?
- Am I in good enough physical condition to handle this attacker?
- Does my attacker NOT have a weapon?
- Is there no chance to escape without using force?

You should also consider the following:
- any personal knowledge you have of your attacker
- any verbal threat the attacker has made
- the attacker's overall behavior
- the area and time of day

you do, keep giving the offensive force your 100 percent effort and do not stop, because **if you hesitate, you may lose that element of surprise**. Use the weapons you will learn about in this book. Use them however you can to stay aggressive and committed to survival until the attacker is no longer a threat and you can escape safely.

The Offensive Mindset

When you face a threat of serious injury or death with no chance to escape, your mindset must become offensive. If you recognize the threat early enough you can strike first to prevent the attack from becoming a self-defense situation. **If you try to stay defensive, you allow your attacker(s) to control the fight.** Try to stay as relaxed as possible; don't let fear freeze your movements or allow your adrenaline to stress you out; try to breathe and use your brain to stay focused on what is happening around you. Technique is not as important as contact in a fight: your technique will not be pretty, but you must make contact with your attacker(s) to be effective. All techniques must be simple, reflexive-instinctive, and work under extreme stress to be effective.

> ## Parameters for use of force
>
> *Deadly force* may be used when a person reasonably believes that the action is necessary for the preservation of human life or to prevent serious physical injury, and when no other reasonable alternatives exist.
>
> *Non-deadly force* may be used in self-defense, or to defend another person from bodily harm.

By striking first, fast and hard you have a good chance of ending the fight before it can begin. **Always try to end the fight as soon as possible** to avoid any chance of serious injury or even death. By taking the offensive in an attack

Seven Common Sense Ways to Survive an Attack

1. Act rather than react.
2. Lead rather than follow.
3. Use offense rather than defense.
4. Strike rather than block.
5. Be decisive rather than hesitate.
6. Succeed rather than give up.
7. Think rather than fight.

you can keep the element of surprise and hopefully control the situation. Don't stop the offensive force until the attacker(s) are no longer a threat, and you can escape safely. Once you decide to take the offensive give it your 100% effort, because if you hesitate you may lose the opportunity of surprise. Use different striking techniques against your attacker(s), stay aggressive and commit to surviving.

Things to Remember:

Remember; you will have to justify the level of force you used according to level of threat and immediate knowledge of the threat at the time of the threat. **Always attempt to avoid any confrontations. Contact the police instead whenever possible.** Any use of force can result in criminal charges against you or civil liability in the future. Check with you local police department, if you have any questions about the use of force.

Armed Attackers: This book is focused on unarmed combat only! Armed combat is a completely different situation and requires even greater skills. The best defense against armed attackers is distance, so create space between you and the attacker. Run; either flee or seek cover. An attacker doesn't need any training or skill to stab you with a kitchen knife, hit you on the head with a club or bottle, or shoot you with a gun. Unless there is an immediate threat of serious injury or death, **I do not recommend that you engage an attacker with a weapon**.

With thanks to the Annapolis Police Department's
General Order Manual, 2001

Rule #1: Use Your Head

Rule #2: Avoid Danger

Rule #3: Know When to Use Force

Rule #4: Know How to Hit

Rule #5: Know What to Hit

Rule #6: Know How to Fight

Rule #7: Train for Self-Defense

Choose Your Weapon

When you're fighting for your life, every move counts. Throw a weak punch or land a kick in the wrong spot and you won't disable your attacker—you'll just make him angrier. Don't take chances. Master the techniques in this section, and every time you hit your opponent, it will hurt. And, while he's doubled over in pain, you can make your escape and save your skin.

If you haven't studied martial arts, this section is especially important, because the techniques it teaches provide you with an alternative to the traditional fist. You'll learn to use your elbows and knees, your head and your hands, your fingers and your feet to achieve your objective: escape with your life.

What's Wrong with the Traditional Fist?

Many people think of the traditional fist when they think of physical fighting. We do not recommend throwing punches—especially to the head—with a closed fist, since the hand can easily break. It takes many hours of practice to learn how to throw an effective punch; even then, you risk injuring yourself. Even Mike Tyson, former boxing heavyweight champion of the world, once broke his hand while hitting without boxing gloves!

So learn these alternatives to the traditional fist, starting with the most powerful of them all: the Hammer Fist.

WEAPON #1-HAMMER FIST

How to make a hammer fist: Roll your fingers tightly into each other and place your thumb against your bent fingers. Use the side of the fist, NOT the knuckles, to strike the body.

Striking Area: Meaty side of the fist below the pinky finger.

Target for the hammer punch: Face, collarbone, ear and groin (from behind).

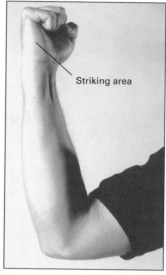

Correct Hammer Fist: No space between fingers; thumb out; wrist straight]

WEAPON #2—HEEL PALM

Use the meaty portion of your hand (just below the middle of your palm) in an upward thrust to the attacker's jaw, nose, or head. Be careful not to strike with your fingers.

How to make the heel palm: Bend your hand back at the wrist. Curl your fingers tightly so that your fingertips just reach the bottom of your fingers.

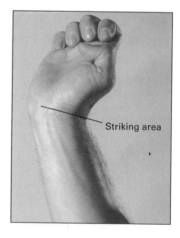

Tuck your thumb in tightly against your hand so that it does not get caught on something and break when throwing this punch.

Striking area: Meaty side of the palm just below the middle of the palm

Target for the heel palm: Primarily face, jaw, and nose.

WEAPON #3—FINGER RAKE/JAB

How to execute the finger rake: Hold your fingers tightly together and slightly bent at the knuckles.

Striking area: Nails and fingertips, or thumb when jabbing.

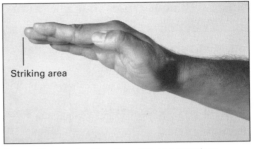

Correct finger rake: thumb and fingers together

Target for the finger rake: Eyes only. This could cause serious injury or blindness. Practice only on a punching bag, not on your workout partner.

WEAPON #4—EAR SLAP

Used correctly, the ear slap will force air into the ear canal, puncturing the eardrums. This can cause dizziness and loss of equilibrium in your attacker.

How to use the ear slap: Cup your hand, bend your fingers at the knuckles, and place your thumb tightly against your hand.

Striking area: Palm of the cupped hand.

Target for the ear slap: one or both ears. When practicing, do not slap your workout partner's ears. Instead, use your partner's shoulders or a punching bag to train with this technique.

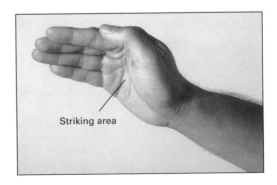

WEAPON #5—OPEN HANDSTRIKE

This technique causes your attacker to choke. This could also kill an attacker by collapsing his windpipe. It is therefore considered deadly force, and should be used only if life is threatened. When using the open handstrike, it is important to position the hand correctly to avoid breaking bones.

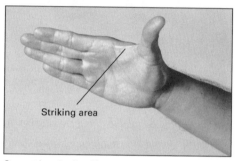

Correct handstrike: Fingers together

How to execute the handstrike: Make your thumb form a V with your fingers. Forcefully thrust the V of your hand into the attacker's throat.

Striking Area: The V formed by your thumb and index finger.

Target for the handstrike: Throat. Train by hitting your work out partner's forearm. Never practice this technique on your partner's throat.

WEAPON #6—HEAD BUTT

How to use the head butt: Tilt your head down, bend your knees slightly, and keep your eyes on your target area–the face. Position yourself closer if possible. Thrust upward with your legs, pushing the top of your head into the attacker's face. If possible, pull the attacker into your head as you grab his arms.

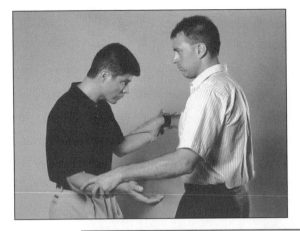

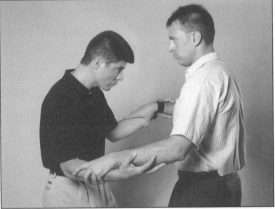

Striking area: Top of the head (not the forehead).

Target for the head butt: The face. Use pads to practice. Grab the pads and pull them to the top of your head.

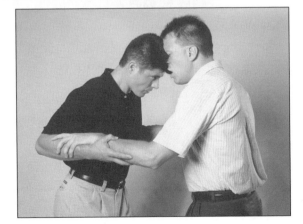

WEAPON #7—BITE

Biting is an excellent way to get a grappler off of you. After the bite, your attacker will try to create space and distance between you. Biting should be used as a last resort. You don't want someone else's blood in your mouth in this day and age of diseases. However, in a life or death situation, biting can give you the break you need in order to escape.

How to bite: Don't use all of your teeth. Instead, angle your face to apply pressure with the incisors. Hold your attacker while you bite to prevent him from pulling away before you bite.

Striking area: Teeth, especially the incisors.

Target for the bite: You can use your teeth on just about any part of your attacker's body, but target areas sensitive to pain. Pick your target: neck, ear, face, stomach, arm, leg, or groin.

WEAPON #8—ELBOW STRIKE

This requires you to be very close to your attacker, so only use an elbow strike if the distance between you has been closed by either you or your attacker. Your elbow is a much harder weapon than your hand.

How to use the elbow strike: Strike your attacker with the tip of your elbow. Use your free arm to block.

Striking Area: The tip of the elbow.

Target of the elbow strike: Unlimited targets include the chin, the face, the neck, the head, and the groin (from behind).

Striking area

WEAPON #9—KNEE STRIKE

How to use the knee strike: Lift the knee no higher than thigh-height, parallel to the floor, to maintain balance. Strike forward, at your attacker's lower body.

Striking area: Top of the knee

Target of the knee strike: Groin, leg or stomach. Practice with a pad or in the air. Use your partner to practice the motion of pulling your attacker into your knee.

WEAPON #10—FOOT STOMP

How to use the foot stomp: Use the heel of your foot (especially a high heel) to slam down on your attacker's foot or scrape his shin.

Striking area: Heel.

Target for the foot stomp: Foot or shin.

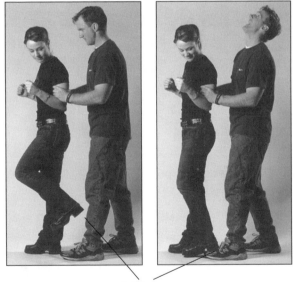

Train by placing a shoe on ground to stimulate the attacker's foot.

WEAPON #11—LOW KICK

This is an effective technique for hitting your attacker's knees or shins.

How to use the low kick:

Place your lead (non-kicking) leg forward. For added power, try to aim the toe of your lead foot in the direction of the kick.

Swing your kicking leg forward and around, keeping it slightly bent.

Strike target area with the inside top of the kicking foot.

Striking Area: Inside top of the foot.

Target of the low kick: knees, shins, or groin. Train with a pad at knee level

WEAPON #12—GROIN KICK

How to use the groin kick: Kick your attacker in the groin. Step into the kick as if you were kicking a door down.

Striking area: Foot, leg, or knee

Target of the groin kick: The groin. Train with a pad at knee level.

Choose Your Target

The most powerful punch in the world is useless unless it hits the intended target. CSSD requires that the effectiveness of your hitting technique be linked to the vulnerable points of the human anatomy. Targets of the body include: hair, temple, nose, ear, eye, throat, neck, shoulder, elbow, fingers, wrist, ribs, stomach, kidney, spine, groin, thigh, knee, behind knee, shin and foot.

Target Vulnerable Areas

Now that you've learned to use the hard parts of your body as weapons, you need to know what parts of the body are vulnerable, and make good targets.

The groin, the knees, the throat, the nose, and the eyes are all areas of the body that no one can toughen up. No matter how big or tough your opponent thinks he is, you will get a response when you strike one of these vulnerable areas.

If your attacker has piercings, they are targets too! Yanking out nose rings, earrings, etc., can be a very effective counterattack.

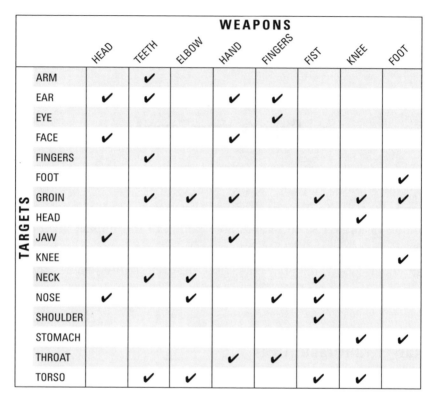

	WEAPONS							
TARGETS	HEAD	TEETH	ELBOW	HAND	FINGERS	FIST	KNEE	FOOT
ARM		✔						
EAR	✔	✔		✔	✔			
EYE					✔			
FACE	✔			✔				
FINGERS		✔						
FOOT								✔
GROIN		✔	✔	✔		✔	✔	✔
HEAD							✔	
JAW	✔			✔				
KNEE								✔
NECK		✔	✔			✔		
NOSE	✔		✔		✔	✔		
SHOULDER						✔		
STOMACH							✔	✔
THROAT				✔	✔			
TORSO		✔	✔			✔	✔	

Each column has a weapon and the recommended targets for a weapon. When you strike, always use at least two or three weapons in combination until you have neutralized the threat.

Putting It Together

So you've practiced your hitting and you've memorized the targets of the body—can that really prepare you for a real-life combat situation? Not entirely. There's one step left: you need to learn to use your knowledge in a realistic and effective way. In this chapter, you'll practice applying your skills in a variety of situations. Once you've tried these with a partner, you'll have a much better idea of how the *Common Sense Self-Defense* rules fit together in actual fight situations—and you should be much more confident in your ability to combat an attacker forcefully enough to escape with your life!

Keep It Simple:

When it comes to fighting, the more complicated the technique, the greater the likelihood that it will fail. Your technique must rely on gross motor skills–you won't always have time to think about your moves if you are suddenly attacked. Use simple techniques that are fast and hard-hitting to survive a fight.

ATTACK #1—DOUBLE ARM GRAB WITH HEAD BUTT

If the attacker grabs both of your arms **(1)**, immediately drive the top of your head into the attacker's face to loosen his hold on you. Never strike using your forehead. Use only the top of your head. Use your legs to thrust upward to increase the power of your head butt. **(2)** Follow up with a knee strike to the groin. **(3, 4)**

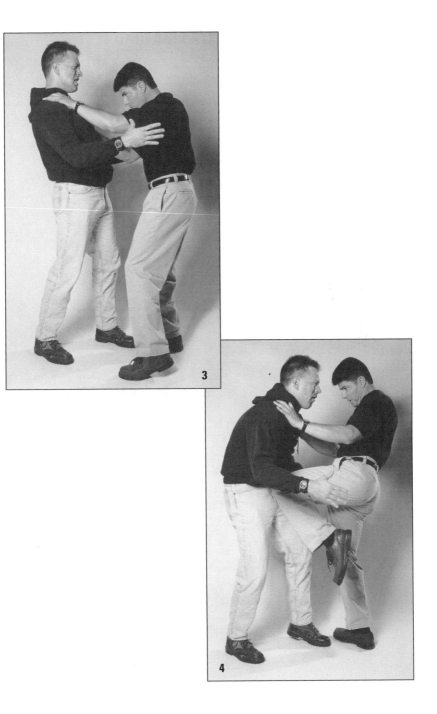

3

4

ATTACK #2—REAR BEAR HUG WITH REAR HEAD BUTT

If the attacker grabs you from behind, be sure to look back and identify him as an attacker. **(1)** Immediately strike the attacker's face with the back of your head to loosen his grip. **(2)** Stomp the attacker's foot. **(3)** Turn and get out of there, or apply another weapon if needed. See Attack #5 or Attack #6 for more ideas.

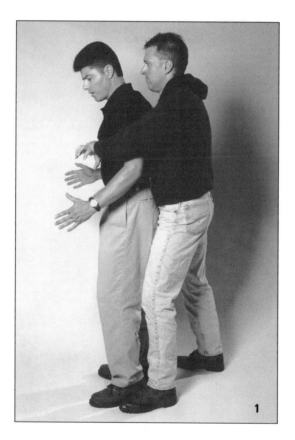

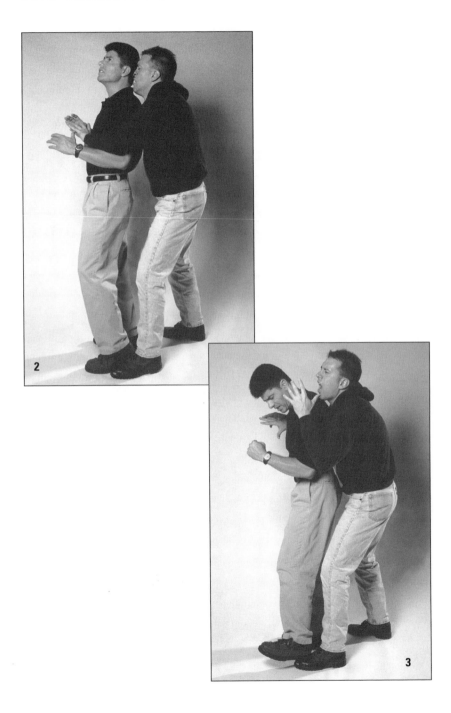

ATTACK #3—HEADLOCK WITH BITE

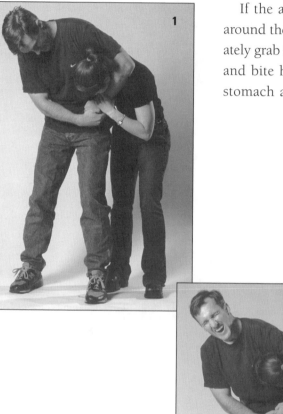

If the attacker grabs you around the head (1) immediately grab the attacker's torso and bite him in the ribs or stomach area to loosen his grip. **(2)** Strike the attacker's groin with a hammer strike. **(3)** Then push your attacker away and run for it. **(4)**

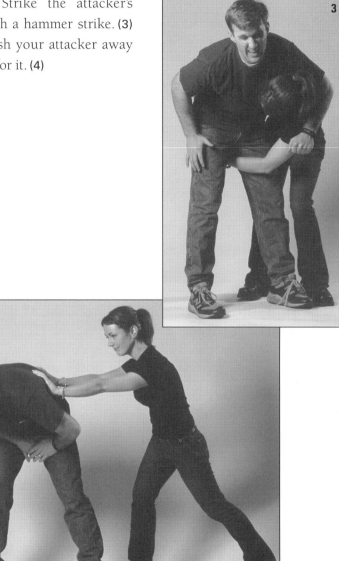

Seven CSSD Fighting Tactics

1. Protect your centerline, from the top of your head to your groin. When fighting, turn your body away from your attacker(s). Your head is the attacker's primary target, so protect it.
2. Strike in a straight line (the shortest distance), using your lead arm or leg.
3. Exert forward pressure.
4. Stay mobile. Don't become a stationary target.
5. Use simple techniques. Pick three to five techniques that work for you. Stay away from flashy or complicated moves.
6. Try to relax. Breathing regularly conserves your energy by increasing your air flow. Relaxing will increase your speed and endurance.
7. Mix up your attack. Use different techniques such as elbow strikes and knee kicks. Don't become predictable.

ATTACK #4—FRONT ATTACK WITH ELBOW STRIKE

If the attacker threatens to injure you, (1) elbow strike the attacker's face (2) and follow up with a front kick to the attacker's groin. (3).

ATTACK #5—REAR ATTACK WITH ELBOW STRIKE AND HEEL PALM

If the attacker grabs you from behind, make sure you identify him as an attacker. (1) Immediately elbow strike the attacker in the face. (2) Then follow up with a heel palm to the attacker's chin. (3)

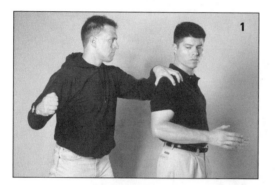

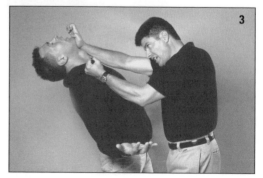

ATTACK #6—REAR ATTACK WITH HAMMER FIST

If the attacker grabs you from behind, be sure to identify him as an attacker. (1) Immediately strike your attacker's groin with the rear hammer fist (2) to loosen his grip. Then pivot, turn away, and escape.

ATTACK #7—FRONT GRAB OR PUSH WITH EAR SLAP AND
LOW KICK

If the attacker grabs you by your shirt or jacket (1), immediately ear slap the attacker to loosen his grip. (2) Then apply a low kick to the attacker's knees (3) followed by a hammer fist to his face or neck. (4)

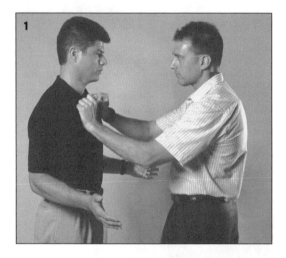

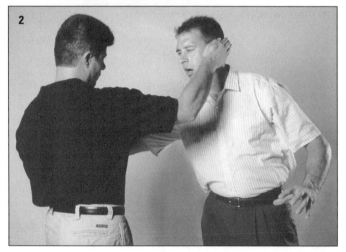

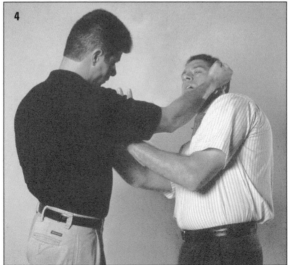

ATTACK #8—FRONT
CHOKE WITH OPEN
HANDCHOP

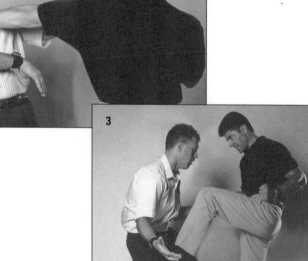

If the attacker grabs you by the neck (1), immediately use an open handstrike to the attacker's neck to break his hold. (2) Then use a front kick to the attacker's groin (3), an elbow strike to his face (4), or a knee to his groin. (5)

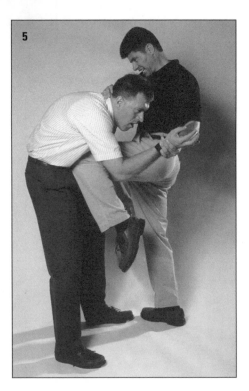

ATTACK #9—ONE-ARM GRAB WITH EYE RAKE

If the attacker grabs your wrist or arm (1), immediately use your free hand to jab the attacker's eye with an eye rake. (2) Then use an elbow strike to the attacker's head (3), followed by a hammer fist to his face (4) and a low kick to his knees if needed. (5)

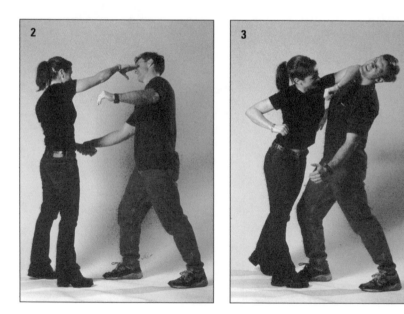

Physical Contact

If forced to fight physically, resist, escape and live.

CONSIDER ESCAPE. Run if you can. There is nothing wrong with escaping to avoid potential injury.

GET CONTROL OF YOURSELF. Breathe, recognize the situation, believe in yourself, and take appropriate action.

SPEAK. Keep using verbal skills such as "Stay Away!" or "Don't come any closer!"

DISTANCE YOURSELF. Maintain a safe distance at all times.

ANALYZE. Start looking for striking points immediately.

POSITION YOURSELF.

- Protect your centerline, from the top of the head to the groin. These are the most vulnerable areas. Attack your opponent's centerline.
- Strike in a straight line; use the shortest distance possible.
- Exert forward pressure. Stay aggressive.
- Stay mobile. Don't be a stationary target.
- Use simple techniques. Pick 3-5 techniques that work well for you; nothing flashy. Mix up your techniques; for example, alternate between hand strikes and kicks.

RELAX. Conserve energy and increase your endurance and speed by staying relaxed.

NEVER GIVE UP. Be committed to defending yourself. There is a lot to say about the power of the mind and never giving up. One thing the military taught us was never to quit under any circumstances. You can use this attitude even if you have no Special Forces training at all. There are many stories about people both young and old who have fought off attackers bigger than them and armed simply because they had the will to live! This "will to live" can take you a long way when defending yourself in a life and death situation.

ATTACK #10—FRONT ATTACK WITH LOW KICK

If the attacker approaches you in a threatening manner (1), keep your hands up to slow or stop the attacker's punch. Immediately kick the attacker's knees (inside or outside) and, if possible, pivot your non-kicking foot in the direction of the kick for added power. Keep your kicking leg slightly bent and swing through the kick. (2) Follow up with an ear slap. (3)

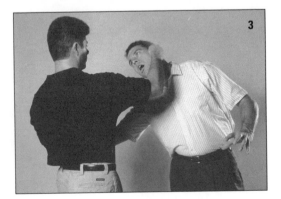

ATTACK #11—ON YOUR BACK WITH EYE RAKE AND EAR SLAP

If the attacker has you on your back (1), immediately eye rake the attacker to loosen his grip and disorient him. (2) Follow up with an ear slap to further disorient him. (3) As you pull your hand across, use your legs to roll the attacker off of you. (4, 5) Being on the ground with your attacker is a very bad situation. You are extremely vulnerable. If you have to, grab and bite the attacker until he gets off of you.

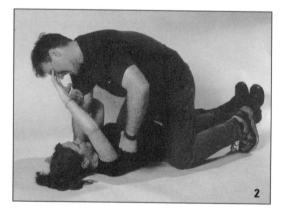

ATTACK #12—TWO ATTACKERS WITH HAMMER FIST AND KNEE STRIKE

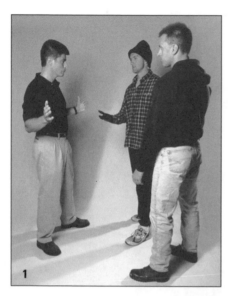

1

If two attackers threaten to hurt you (1), immediately strike the closest attacker with a hammer fist to the face or neck. (2) Follow up with a knee strike to the attacker's groin, chest, or head. (3) Always try to keep the attacker you strike first between you and the other attacker as a shield. (4) Leave the area immediately. (5)

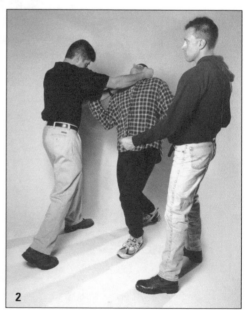

2

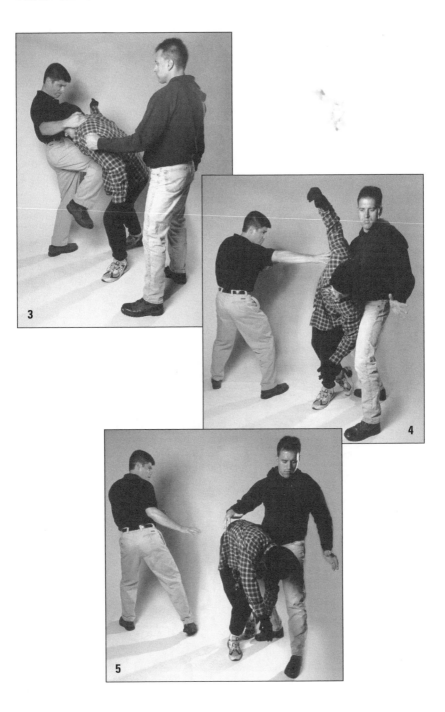

Use Whatever You Can; Do Whatever It Takes

If your life is in danger, exploit your environment; use anything and everything at your disposal to make yourself safe again. If you're carrying a book bag or a purse, use it. If a chair is nearby, use it. If you're holding a cup of coffee, a fire extinguisher, or car keys, use them. Almost every environment contains something that you can use as a weapon or a shield.

Rule #1: Use Your Head

Rule #2: Avoid Danger

Rule #3: Know When to Use Force

Rule #4: Know How to Hit

Rule #5: Know What to Hit

Rule #6: Know How to Fight

Rule #7: Train for Self-Defense

Why Train?

If you ever find yourself in a situation where you need to use the techniques outlined in this book, you will not have time to think. Fear and panic, coupled with the need to act instantly, mean that all your knowledge of self-defense must be automatic. **You will not learn these techniques just by reading about them.** Only by physically repeating the movements will you make them second nature, so you can use them when you need them most. You need to commit these motions to muscle memory in order to avoid letting fear take over and freeze your movements in the event of a real attack.

In addition to reacting instantly, you must also be able to react powerfully. That's why we recommend that you follow a basic fitness program to maintain good physical fitness. By keeping in shape, you will have the strength and endurance you need to resist an attack—or, even better, to run away from it and avoid it altogether.

Train Hard, Fight Easy

The harder you train, the better your chance of surviving a fight. Use realistic training scenarios, and push yourself to 100% effort. When you train, wear the clothing you normally wear, whether it's blue jeans, a suit, or a dress. Try different techniques using both your strong hand/foot and your weak hand/foot. Of course, practicing the techniques cannot guarantee success, but it will leave you better prepared for an attack.

How Should I Train?

The best way to train in the CSSD way is to practice with a partner or to take a class lead by a certified CSSD instructor.

Each of the hitting techniques can be practiced with minimal equipment at your local gym. You will need these supplies found at a martial arts supply store.

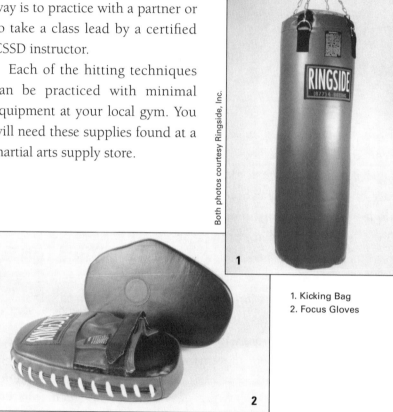

Both photos courtesy Ringside, Inc.

1. Kicking Bag
2. Focus Gloves

How Often Should I Train?

Until you master these techniques, train several times a week. Repeat the movements described in the "Know How to Hit" section of this book, and practice the combinations outlined in "Know How to Fight." When you feel very comfortable with both of these skills, practice once a week to maintain your abilities.

Maintaining Basic Fitness

Stay in good physical condition. Staying fit increases your self-confidence and your physical presence. Fitness helps relieve daily stress, helps prevent injury, and makes you feel better about yourself. Sufficient fitness along with proper nutrition and rest is will keep you at your best. The Surgeon General recommends exercising at least 3 times a week for at least 20 minutes.

Some activities you might try include running, swimming, biking, or aerobics classes. Also include strength (resistance) training with light weights.

Some excellent resources for fitness training are listed below:

BOOKS

Maximum Fitness
    A challenging cross-training fitness program.
The Official Navy SEAL Workout
    Great workouts for men and women who want to train without
    weights.
The Body Sculpting Bibles for Men and Women
    A total resource for weight training.
Combat Fat!
    Weight loss and exercise program.

VIDEOS

The Boot Camp Workout Videos
    Basic and Advanced training provides follow-along workouts for
    home use.

WEB

GetFitNow.com

   Destination site for men and women who want the best in fitness, exercise, and nutrition information. Forums, articles, on-
   line store are featured.

About the Authors

Dave Garcia (left)
and Stew Smith
(right)

Dave Garcia

Dave Garcia has been a Police Officer in the state of Maryland for the past 12 years. During that time, he has had the opportunity to refine his hand-to-hand combat skills in well over 1,000 arrests. Before joining the Police force, Dave was a sergeant in the U.S. Marine Corps Special Forces, and served in the U.S. Army in the 11th Group Special Forces. He is a Certified Law Enforcement instructor in Krav Maga, level 1, as well as a black belt in 1st Dan Taekwondo and an expert in Jeet Kune Do. His skills have served him well in Level 1 Special Combat Aggressive Reactionary training System (SCARS), SWAT counter-sniper/hostage rescue training, and as an actor/stuntman for the live-action Batman 2000 Thrill Spectacular and 2001 show at Six Flags of America.

Stew Smith

Stew Smith graduated from the U.S. Naval Academy in 1991 and served for eight years as a U. S. Navy SEAL. At the Naval Academy, he has taught Judo, self-defense, and the Navy SEAL Prep Course. Like Dave, he has participated in SCARS Level 1 training. In addition to working as a fitness columnist for military.com, Stew has authored numerous books, including *The Complete Guide to Navy SEAL Fitness* and *The TV Watcher's Workout*.